High Five
HENRY

Alan MacDonald

Illustrated by
Philippe Dupasquier

O2
UNI

D1335896

OXFORD
UNIVERSITY PRESS

Great Clarendon Street, Oxford, OX2 6DP,
United Kingdom

Oxford University Press is a department of the University of Oxford.
It furthers the University's objective of excellence in research, scholarship,
and education by publishing worldwide. Oxford is a registered trade mark of
Oxford University Press in the UK and in certain other countries

Text © Alan MacDonald 2002

The moral rights of the author have been asserted

First published in this edition 2016

British Library Cataloguing in Publication Data
Data available

978-0-19-837716-0

7 9 10 8

Paper used in the production of this book is a natural, recyclable product
made from wood grown in sustainable forests. The manufacturing process
conforms to the environmental regulations of the country of origin.

Printed in India by Manipal Technologies Limited

Acknowledgements
Cover and inside illustrations by Philippe Dupasquier
Inside cover notes written by Sasha Morton

Contents

Chapter 1
Famous Henry

Henry is our school lollipop man. He's famous. He's probably the most famous lollipop man there is.

Let me tell you how it all started.

My name's Alex and Mo is my little sister. Her real name's Milly, but I call her Mo. She's so small she only comes up to my chest.

Mo likes Henry. In fact, everyone in our school likes him. Henry never forgets your name. He never asks you silly questions like, "How was school today?"

But the best thing about Henry is the way that he greets you. Other lollipop men probably say, "Good morning" or just "Hello." Henry is different. He gives high fives.

No one knows how the high fives first started. Damon Shaw says he was the first one to give Henry a high five. Then Henry copied him. But Damon also reckons the Queen is his grandma, so nobody believes him.

Me, I think Henry just did it because he felt like it. He stood in the road with his lollipop stick. As someone went past, he said, "Gimme five!"

And they did. They slapped his hand. Then the next person to cross wanted a high five. That's how it began. Henry probably didn't know what he was starting that day. Now, nobody in our school crosses the road without a high five from Henry.

At least, nobody did until the day Henry got the letter. That's the story I want to tell you.

Chapter 2
The Bulldog in the Car

It was a Monday morning. I was
walking to school with Mo and Zac.
Zac is my best friend. (He's also the
biggest dreamer I know. Once, he came
to school wearing his pyjama top under
his sweater. I had to swear not to tell
anyone.)

Anyway, Henry was waiting by the
road with his lollipop, as usual.

There were six or seven of us waiting to cross. Henry stepped into the middle of the road. He held out his lollipop to stop the traffic.

As we crossed, Henry held out his hand. He said, "Gimme five."

We all slapped his hand and said, "Hi, Henry!" or "Morning, Henry!"

But that morning, Mo somehow got missed out.

It wasn't until we got across the road that I noticed she'd gone quiet. Her bottom lip was wobbling.

"Henry!" I called out. "You missed Mo!"

"Oh, Mo. I'm sorry!" he said, and beckoned her to come back.

While we all watched, he gave Mo a special. (One high five, one low five, one behind the back.)

Mo ran back to me. She was beaming all over her face. "I got a Henry special," she grinned.

By this time, a big blue car was hooting its horn. Then the owner got out. He was a big man with a face that looked like an angry bulldog.

"What do you think you're doing?" he asked Henry loudly.

"What do you mean?" asked Henry, blinking through his glasses.

"I mean, why are you holding up the traffic? We're sitting here waiting while you play games with little kids."

Henry looked surprised. "I always do that. The children like it."

"Well, I *don't* like it," said the man. He pushed his big face into Henry's. "I don't like you keeping me waiting. I'll be making a complaint."

By now, there were about ten cars all tooting their horns. Henry was looking very upset. Bulldog got back into his car, slammed the door and drove off. It was all over quickly. I went into school and forgot about it – until the following Friday. That's when Henry began acting oddly.

Chapter 3
The Letter

Zac, Mo and I were crossing the road. I held out my hand to give Henry a big high five, as I passed.

"Hi, Henry!"

"Morning," said Henry, gloomily. He didn't take his hand out of his pocket.

"Hey, Henry! Gimme five!" I said.

"Sorry, I can't," said Henry.

I stopped. "Why not? Something wrong with your hand?"

"I'm not allowed. Quick, cross the road. Or you'll get me into more trouble."

Henry took us over and trudged back to his place on the pavement. I'd never seen him look so miserable.

"What's wrong with Henry?" asked Mo in a small voice. "I didn't get a high five."

"I know, Mo," I said. "Nor did I."

"He didn't even smile!" said Zac. When Zac notices something is wrong, it has to be serious.

In the playground, all the other kids were talking about the same thing. What was wrong with Henry? Why wasn't he giving high fives?

Just then, the bell went for the start of school. I looked back at Henry. He was helping another group of children across the road. They held out their hands for a high five. But he shook his head sadly. Something was very wrong.

After school we went to see Henry.

"What's up?" I asked.

Without a word, Henry took a letter
out of his pocket. He handed it to us.
It said:

Dear Mr Little,
(that was Henry's name)

A serious complaint has been
made about you.

Please do not slap children on
the hand as they cross the road.
For one thing, it holds up the
traffic. For another, it could be
dangerous. You should watch the
road at all times. If you carry on in
this way, I will be forced to take
further action.

Yours sincerely,

Hazel Ryan

Hazel Ryan
Council Services

"What's that mean: 'further action'?"
asked Zac.

"It means they'll give me the boot.
Kick me out," said Henry.

"They can't do that!" I said.

"We won't let 'em kick you!" said Mo,
screwing up her little fists.

"There's nothing you can do," said
Henry. "I just have to stop the high fives,
that's all."

"But we *like* your high fives," said Zac. "They're cool."

"They're funny," said Mo.

"I know," said Henry. "I feel like I'm letting everyone down."

I gave Henry back the letter.

"Don't worry. We'll think of something," I said.

I sounded confident, but what could we do? We were just a bunch of school kids. Who was going to listen to us?

Chapter 4
Operation Lollipop

"We could draw up a thingy," said Zac. "One of those lists. You know … with all our names. It's … we sign our names and —"

"You mean a petition," said someone.

I'd called a meeting in the playground. There were about ten of us from my class. Plus Mo. If it was about Henry, she wasn't going to be left out.

"A petition won't do any good," I said. "People are always starting petitions. We need to do something."

"I know," said Damon Shaw. "I can do it. I'll stand next to Henry. I'll give everyone a high five for him."

There was a silence.

"Just an idea," said Damon.

"We could wear badges," said
Beth Sims, "badges that say: 'We
like Henry's high fives! We want them
back!'"

"You'd never get all that on a badge," I
pointed out.

"Well, I'm going on … you know …
I'm going on … strike," said Zac.

"Unless Henry does his high fives, I'm not
doing my homework."

Everybody laughed. Zac never did his homework anyway. He always forgot. But he'd set me thinking. A strike. It might just work. It was a crazy idea, but crazy ideas are sometimes the best.

We didn't tell Henry about our plan. He would have tried to stop us. All weekend, we talked about nothing but Operation Lollipop. That was our code name for it.

Chapter 5
On Strike

On Monday morning, we put our plan into action. Mo, Zac and I set out for school early.

"Know what to do?" I whispered, as we spotted Henry. They both nodded.

"Morning," said Henry. He gave us a cheery smile and we all smiled back. He held out his lollipop to stop the cars. The three of us started to cross.

"Gimme five, Henry!" shouted Mo, holding up her hand.

"Don't," groaned Henry. "You'll get me into trouble."

Then we did it. We stopped in the middle of the road. And we didn't budge.

Henry stared at us, amazed. "Go on, then. What are you waiting for?"

"A high five," I said. "We're not moving till you give us one."

Henry looked worried. He looked over our heads at the traffic.

"Alex!" he hissed. "You'll get me the boot. Cross the road."

"We can't," said Zac firmly. "We're on ... thingy."

"Strike," I said. "We're on strike till the council lets you do your high fives."

Another group of children joined us in the middle of the road.

"Over you go," said Henry.

They shook their heads. They all knew about Operation Lollipop.

There were now six cars waiting. I could see a bus coming this way. More children joined us. We made a line stretching right across the road.

The bus stopped. The driver leaned out of his window.

"Hey!" he shouted. "Get those kids out the road!"

Henry took off his hat and scratched his head.

"Look," he said to me in a low voice. "I know you're trying to help, but this won't do any good."

"Why not?" I said. "If they want us to move, they'll have to give in. Won't they?"

At nine o'clock, the bell rang. But the playground was empty. Every child in the school was standing in the middle of the road, blocking the traffic.

In both directions, cars stretched as far back as we could see.

Some drivers were arguing with Henry. Others had got out of their cars and were arguing with each other.

The rest had turned on their radios and were making the best of the wait.

At ten past nine, Mrs Minton our headteacher came striding across the playground. We could tell she was angry. When Mrs Minton's angry, her voice can stop a charging rhino in its tracks.

"Look out," I whispered to Zac. "Here she comes."

"What is going on?" demanded Mrs Minton. She was facing Henry.

"I'm sorry," said Henry. "It's not my idea, Mrs Minton. I've asked them to move. But they won't."

"All of you. Out of the road, this minute!" ordered Mrs Minton.

Some of the younger children looked ready to run. The older ones looked at me. It was my idea, so they expected me to do the explaining. I opened my mouth. Nothing came out.

It was Mo who spoke up.

"Henry's got to high five us," she said in her breathless little voice.

"Who said that? Was that you, Milly?" asked Mrs Minton.

"Yes," said Mo. "Henry's got to give us all a high five. Then we'll go."

"We don't think that letter was fair," I added, finding my voice at last. "So we're on strike. Till the council changes its mind."

"I see," said Mrs Minton. "And you think standing in the middle of the road's going to help Henry?" She wasn't shouting. In fact, she didn't even look angry.

Then the police car arrived.

Chapter 6
Under Arrest

A policeman got out. He walked over to us.

"Who's in charge?" he demanded.

"I'm the headteacher," said Mrs Minton.

"Then move these children off the road, please. They're holding up the traffic."

"I'm sorry," said Mrs Minton. "They are waiting for their lollipop man – that's Henry there – to give them a high five."

"A *what?*" said the policeman.

"A high five," said Henry. "You hold out your hand ... "

"I know what it is!" said the policeman. "So why doesn't he do it?"

"I can't," explained Henry. "The council have banned my high fives. They say they're a danger to road safety."

It was now the policeman's turn to scratch his head. He went back to his car and talked over the radio. Whoever was on the other end didn't sound very pleased.

"Right, that's it," said the policeman. "Either you kids clear the road now, or I'll have to arrest somebody."

"Arrest who?" asked Mrs Minton. "You can't arrest two hundred children!"

The policeman looked flustered.
Then he pointed to Henry. "Him," he
said. "I'll arrest him. He started all
this."

"Henry?" I shouted. "But that's not fair.
Henry didn't do anything!"

The policeman shrugged. "It's up to
you," he said, grimly. "I'll give you ten
seconds to clear the road." He started to
count. "One ... "

I looked at Zac. We wanted to help Henry, but now it looked like we were going to get him arrested. It was no good. We'd have to give in.

" … nine … ten!" counted the policeman.

"Wait!" called a voice. "If you're arresting Henry, you'll have to arrest us, too."

I looked around. A small army of lollipop holders stood on the pavement. It looked like every lollipop holder in the town had come to join our protest.

"How did they get here?" I whispered to Zac.

"I told them," said Zac, grinning. "At least, I told one of them. He must have passed the message on."

"Zac, you're a genius!" I said. "Why didn't you tell me?"

"Forgot," said Zac.

The policeman looked at the lollipop holders. He looked at Henry. He looked at us. "You're all bananas," he said. He went back to his car. "We've got a problem," we heard him mutter into the radio.

41

Chapter 7
High Fives

Half an hour later, Hazel Ryan got out of her car. She looked startled to see hundreds of children blocking the road. A traffic jam stretched away in both directions.

"Are you the woman from the council?" asked the policeman.

"Yes," said Mrs Ryan.

"Did you send this letter?" The policeman waved Henry's letter under her nose.

"Yes, we had a complaint," she replied.

"Well, now *I'm* complaining," said the policeman. "I've got two hundred children, a bunch of teachers and a gang of lollipop holders blocking the road. I've got a traffic jam a mile long and nobody can move. And it's all because you won't let Henry here give his five highs."

"*High fives*," Mo corrected. The policeman glared at her. He turned back to Mrs Ryan. She was looking rather pale.

"You started all this. What are you going to do about it?"

"Well," said Mrs Ryan. "I um ... I must admit I've not seen these high fives myself."

Henry pushed his way through.
"Hold up your hand," he said. Mrs
Ryan shyly did so. Henry gave her a high
five.

"Oh," said Mrs Ryan. "And that's it?"

"That's it," said Henry. "Takes less
than a second. And I can watch the traffic
all the time."

"Does that mean Henry can go on
doing it?" I asked.

There was a pause. Everyone looked at Mrs Ryan.

"Well … " she said at last, "it doesn't seem to do any harm … "

The rest of her words were lost in a huge cheer.

We all surrounded Henry and started giving him high fives. The lollipop army then carried him shoulder-high through the school gates.

The policeman shook Mrs Minton's hand. Even the drivers hooted their horns as the mile-long traffic jam moved off down the road.

That was how Henry got his high fives back. Life soon got back to normal again at school – although I hear it's starting to spread. Next time a lollipop holder helps you across the road, get ready for the high five!

About the author

Believe it or not, this story is based on something I read in a newspaper.

The report said a local council had banned a lollipop man from giving high fives to school children. This seemed so daft to me that it was perfect material for a story. I sat down and wrote *High Five Henry.*

Maybe, one day, the real-life Henry will read the story and recognize himself!